Perfume of the Unwritten

Also by the author

Lights of Yearning: In Praise of the Most Praised ﷺ

The Secret of Divine Alchemy: In Praise of the Most Beloved ﷺ

Title: Perfume of the Unwritten

Author: Walid Lounès Bouzerar
Foreword by: H.E. Shaykh Nour Hisham Kabbani

Editor: Abdul Aziz Suraqah
Book designer & typesetter: Walid Lounès Bouzerar
Publisher: Dar al-Habib

Paperback: 978-0-9948107-5-5
Hardcover: 978-0-9948107-6-2

www.lounesthepoet.com
www.daralhabib.com
www.facebook.com/perfumeoftheunwritten

بِسْمِ ٱللَّهِ ٱلرَّحْمَٰنِ ٱلرَّحِيمِ

In loving memory of

Sayyidinā al-Shaykh Muḥammad ibn al-Ḥabīb
al-Amghārī al-Idrīssī al-Ḥassanī

May Allāh sanctify his secret
& benefit us through his knowledge and mention

﴿الَّذِينَ يَذْكُرُونَ اللَّهَ قِيَامًا وَقُعُودًا وَعَلَىٰ جُنُوبِهِمْ
وَيَتَفَكَّرُونَ فِي خَلْقِ السَّمَاوَاتِ وَالْأَرْضِ
رَبَّنَا مَا خَلَقْتَ هَٰذَا بَاطِلًا سُبْحَانَكَ
فَقِنَا عَذَابَ النَّارِ ﴿١٩١﴾﴾

Those who remember Allāh,
standing and sitting and on their sides,
and reflect upon the creation of the heavens and the earth:
'Our Lord, Thou hast not created this for vanity.
Glory be to Thee!
Guard us against the chastisement of the Fire.'

Qur'ān 3:191

PERFUME OF THE UNWRITTEN

Poetry & Prose by
Walid Lounès Bouzerar

Foreword by
H.E. Shaykh Nour Hisham Kabbani

Contents

Introduction

All praise is due to Allāh, the Lord of the Worlds, and may His Infinite Divine Peace and Blessings shower *the Coolness of our Eye*, *our Guide to the Truth, the Solace of our Souls,* who was named *the Most Praised,* for he is the most praised in creation throughout the Heavens and the Earth, *the Most Honoured, the Most Majestic, the Most Beautiful, the Most Perfect, the Most Beloved, our Master, Abū al-Qāṣim,* he is *Muḥammad,* son of ʿAbdullāh son of ʿAbd ul-Muṭṭalib son of Hāshim, and may this prayer of peace and blessings be extended to his sanctified family, *our Lady* Fāṭimat ul-Zahrāʾ, *our Master* and *Star of Guidance, the Lion of Allāh,* ʿAlī son of Abū Ṭālib, their blessed sons *the Martyrs* al-Ḥassan and al-Ḥusayn, and their entire Holy Progeny from their Sacred lifetimes until the *Day of Reckoning.*

This is a collection of poetry that I have compiled into a book and I have named it *Perfume of the Unwritten.* It could also be called *Scent of the Inexpressible.* And it could also be called *Aroma of the Hidden*. Or it could also be called *Perfume of the Unmanifest*. And it could also be called *Fragrance of the Veiled.*

These poems were written in a highly transformative period of my life, penned as a medium of counsel to my own self, *by Divine Grace,* through the *Waters of Wisdom* sipped and the Lights in which my Soul was bathed from the Oceans of my *Shuyūkh* and *the Men of Allāh* through interactions with them in waking and non-waking states. I share this collection praying that the transformative manifestation that it was birthed from may touch the reader.

I would like to thank my parents, Farouk and Farida, as well as my sisters for their support, may their lives be long and their Souls be guided and their hearts be tranquil.

I would like to remember *my rope of guidance, pillar of wisdom, beacon of Light, the river extending from the Ocean of Muḥammadan Lights* ﷺ, whose quenching waters of Proximity flow generously of which its cool, refreshing taste and fragrant scent brings life back to the deadened and feeble hearts, he whose character, words and actions provide knowledge of Muḥammad ﷺ, erase our troubles, and open our hearts to visions of the Next World, *our Master* and *Companion,* Moulay Ḥassan al-ʿAlaouī, may Allāh have Mercy on him and his family, be well pleased with him and keep us in his company in this life and the Next and may the prayer extend to his Noble Father-in-law, *the great Qutb, the Mountain amongst men, the Majestic Gnostic and Lover of Allāh Most High, our Master,* Sidna Shaykh Muḥammad Bel Qurshī, and in turn his Shaykh, *the Inheritor of the Muḥammadan Treasures, Possessor of the Station of Shaykh-hood, the Knower of Allāh, our Master,* Sidna Shaykh Muḥammad ibn al-Ḥabīb, may Allāh envelope them all in His Special Mercy and include us with them, and may we benefit from their knowledge and Light in this life and the Next.

The needy of Allāh's Mercy,
Walid Lounès Bouzerar

Foreword

In the Name of Allāh, the Compassionate, the Merciful

Imām Bukhārī cited a ḥadīth of Prophet Muḥammad, Allāh's blessings and peace be upon him, *"Inna min al-shi'ri laḥikmatun." Surely, in poetry there is Wisdom.* Wisdom that denies the victory of ignorance and *Kufr (disbelief).*

According to their stations and destinations, the noble poets walk the *path of spiritual intimacy* through gardens of *Dhikrullāh (remembrance of God)* and *Īmān (faith).* They perpetually seek heavenly connection through a higher understanding that enslaves believers and liberates sinners.

Bathed in *Tawḥīd (Unicity of God)* and *Tafakkur (contemplation),* they are blissfully wrapped in illumined states that elevate their praises of Allāh Almighty and Sayyidinā Muḥammad, *Allāh's blessings and peace be upon him.*

Their attuned hearts are inspired by Angels. Their ethereal entreaties call us to devout obedience and worship, encouraging us to love our Lord and His Beloved, *Allāh's peace and blessings be upon him,* evermore and to unfailingly seek their closeness.

May Allāh, *Exalted be He,* and His Prophet, *Allāh's blessings and peace be upon him,* bless and support you, and may you be granted the company of those noble poets in whose footsteps you follow.

H.E. Shaykh Nour Hisham Kabbani

PERFUME OF THE UNWRITTEN

Poetry & Prose by
Walid Lounès Bouzerar

Foreword by
H.E. Shaykh Nour Hisham Kabbani

Only Kings Do Find

My heart sings a tune
That confounds my mind
Sets its eyes on Gold
Only Kings do find

What Horizons hold
Ever seeks to know
What the Oceans hide
And the Masters know

Burning down the walls
Bringing in the Light
Brighter than the stars
Dancing in the night

"How reckless you are,"
Says reasoning mind.

O how's the dog to know
The sweetness of flight?
Or the shadow to
Taste the Sun's delight?

O my heart, shine on
Singing in the night
O my heart, burn on
Bringing in the Light

My breath shed a sigh
With my limbs at rest
Spoke a thousand lines
That my heart expressed

Pulled a thousand fears
From a broken chest
Sang a thousand songs
From an empty nest

Like an orphaned bird
Wings spread in flight
And a soothing tune
Mingling with the night

Finding solace in
Spreading far this Light
A burning longing
Birthed at night

To a time for change
To a cry for hope
To break from the chains
Of a tightening rope

Burning on the cheek
Of a desert road
On its own to seek
The Endless Abode

Alchemy of the Soul

Windless breeze of Wisdom
Scentless fragrance; timeless, silent rhythm
Hueless prism through which
Seas of meaning pierce through spirits risen

Seekers bloom with states
The lovers soar with no abiding station
Sinners turn to Saints
As golden rays to save the meek and patient

Stillness is its garden
In which seedlings bathe in rays of Presence
Brokenness, its water
Quenching thirsts of those who graze in Essence

Its ocean quenches deserts
Drowned in beauty witnessing its pleasance
Peasants praised by Kings
By their adornment in its sacred dresses

Windless breeze of wisdom
Hidden valley in the hearts of men

A majestic Presence
Like the King inside the lion's den

Roaming every land
In search of hearts for a silent friend
Thirsty souls
Looking to quench their thirsts with the Light
again

Blazing fire drowning
Every shadow that desire sends
Staircase to the Heavens on which
Open inner eyes ascend

Traveling the spectrum
Of hearts' melodies to the higher ends
Healing their broken wings
And watching them *rise again*

People of the Cave

Prayer is better than sleep
Sleep is better than distraction

Silence is better than speech
Except speech brought forth as just action

The lover's heart knows no sleep
Its chambers echo with His Name

His closed eyes are but an umbrella
To veil his state in the pouring rain

Like *the People of the Cave*
The lover darkens his eyes and senses

In loving protection of his heart
Ornamented in Sacred Dresses

His limbs are limp, his eyes are weary
His tongue is frail, his words are few

His heart is blazing in a dark abyss
With glowing eyes set on the True

The lover's deaf to outward reproaches
For his heart is comforted by the Kind

The Subtle pulls his heart to bliss
Into the Light and out of sight

I Forgo My Nest

Is that bird not a fool who, with healthy wings
Matured with bones of sturdy strength
With a vision sharp and new-grown feathers
In its nest decides to stay?

I forgo my nest like the hungry hawk
To attend to my Spirit's nourishment
To the blessed lands of my forefathers
The abode of the chosen Saints

The land well-flooded by the pouring Light
Of the Sons of Pure Descent
The Holy Family of the One
Whose name is *The Most Praised*

Whose station is The Most Raised
We ask for his Intercession
And for his noble Presence
On this day till the Resurrection

And through him we relieve our tension
May he bring us to his blessed Heirs

To their blessed care
And may we be joined in their blessed prayer

My heart like a bee, much too speechless to say
Which flower is sweeter
As Nectar flows freely
From the Presence of the blessed Saints

Those beloved Souls who spread the Light
Who ease the heart, expand the mind
The ardent Lovers I set out to find
Blessed souls in communion with their Beloved
In the recesses of the pitch black night

May our steps be guided, our words be Light
Our witnessing *above mention*
My our hands be held by the Spirit of
Our Guide towards Perfection

May Divine Blessings and Peace be
Upon *The Master of Intercession*
And may his name upon our hearts
Be our *Eternal protection*
Be our every ailment's *Divine Correction*
And grant us *Celestial Mention*

Home

They came in ships and cavalry
That they may eventually land

In a dream-like lush green landscape
The land your fathers built by hand

The worm is drawn to the ripest dates
The night moth drawn to the brightest light

It's in your hands now, what will you make
Of its day following that lengthy night

What is it of its sublime beauty
That your eyes refuse to see?

The forests, mountains, fertile land
The rivers and clear blue sea

The majestic inscribed prayer walls
The colorful smiles of your mothers

The inner light that shines from the hearts
And the eyes of your sisters and brothers

Why does your glance turn to the horizons?
Magnificence is staring at you from close

In the lands of your Saintly fathers
Grow from those ruins like the desert rose

Love-borne Wings

Give your form up to the Formless
At the hand of one dressed in

A celestially-adorned glimpse
His sign, should it be destined

Your inner heart's eyes won't miss
Heavenly-informed bliss

His presence as a *Holy Cloud*
In which every aspiring Soul is rinsed

Elevating the droning melodies
That every worldly storm sings

Calamity transformed to blessings
Raised up by Love-borne wings

The tree only bears fruit
Once it's firmly established roots

Once the soul aims to its Beloved
The actions follow suit

The Elders mine the Gold
After they've sought it in their youth

Once the *inner* Path unfolds
The *outer* favors Truth

The Rose & Its Demise

Such a delicate lifespan
And yet
Despite the arrival of death
The petals of the rose radiate
As an open letter
Her red cheeks blossoming
Manifesting the light of the Sun that feeds her
And the water that quenches her
And the soil that nurtures her
At peace with her inevitable demise to come
Her gratitude unadulterated by it
Her joviality untainted by it
Her celebration uninterrupted by it
It is through this perspective
That even long after her stem has dried
And her roots have been severed
And her thorns made blunt
Her spirit lives in her *fragrance*
Her crimson petals still tasteful
Her sweet-scented oil still an adornment
Praised and sought after earnestly
By peasants and Kings alike

When has the rose ever apologised for
her thorns?
Yet her fragrance is still revered
Her nectar, still sweet
Her beauty, still complete
She has no concern other than being *the rose*
Burning in that bliss
Singing of her *Sower*
Knowing *the praise is His*

The Ocean to Which Every Celestial River Flows

If Love should visit in the night
Hold on to Her Blessed Cloak

From all distractions turn your eyes
Wherever Her Flight takes don't let go

For in Her Presence fire's vanquished
Mountains are crumbled like melting snow

One glance from Her's all it takes
For the *Gardens of the Heart* to grow

The destitute are raised up to the
Highest Skies from the humblest lows

Her Drink is what every Seeker's after
And what every Holy Gnostic knows

Her Fragrance opens feeble hearts
Regardless of how tightly closed

Her petals of *Wisdom* intoxicate
At the tongue's touch with the slightest dose

She's the fastest means the Saints have risen
The Hand that every Yearner chose

For She's the Ocean *to which*
Every Celestial River flows

Love May Come to Pour

Who is more at loss than the dry heart
That sits idle in its unquenched thirst
That *Endless Quenching Fountain* is
With *he* from whom the Secrets burst ﷺ

Don't you see how the *Boundless Ocean*
Calls the *shell* back to where it's from
Only once it's *emptied of itself*
That hypnotic lull of the waves' song
Its *being* filled with its enrapturing tune
'O leave those crowded shores and come'

Always have your cup empty -
Love may come to pour
Keep the path and carpet sparkling
By the open door
When She comes you'll know *Her Fragrance*
From a hundred miles away
Awaiting Her Arrival *is itself*
A silent prayer

The Sea of Why You Do It

Drown the *form* of *what you do*
In the *sea* of *why you do it*

Forget the words and sounds
For innate Love will guide you through it

Your words are your hearts music
Your thoughts the strings you choose

Let that burning Light shine through
Whenever you sing your tunes

Your melody's colored by your state
Watch your heart before you play

That way every note's a prayer
Every breath a step on the Way

Follow the trails that Silence lays
And don't be afraid of the stormy seas

New lands were never discovered
Without heartaches and shaking knees

The storms of fate are sure to come
But the seedlings never shy away

Buried humbly, lightning strikes
Yet sure enough *water comes their way*

Things of This World

The prayer of a drowning man
The fruit in a barren land

The laughter of an orphan child
Compassion in the open wild

The high head of the oppressed
The mercy in a well-fed nest

The standstill patience of the broken
The eloquence of the unspoken

The praise from a want-less heart
The elderly man with a new start

The God-fearing of a just ruler
The *'I don't know'* of a true scholar

A bountiful well in the thirsty sands
The selfless hand of a homeless man

The Rope That Love Sends

We have a lot to say on
What we think about Love
But few take the time to
Listen to what Love says

We go to great lengths to
Be about what friends love
But few care to *seek*
The whereabouts of Love's friends

A friend told me once
'What Love breaks Love does mend'
I add, *seek to be*
That mending hand that Love lends

So reach the *Infinite*
Through the rope that Love sends
For Love has no beginning
And neither does Love end

What Has Your Yearning Brought You?

'O you miserable fool!'
The gathered people reproached Majnūn,
'After all these years in this helpless state,
What has your yearning for Laylā brought you?'

'And what has the flower gained *reaching* to the *Sun?'*
He said,
'What has the drop gained *merging* with the *ocean?*
What has the plume gained *yielding* to the *poet's hand?*
What has the reed gained *surrendering* to the *musician's breath?*
Tell me, what has the *Moon* gained,
O you hearts of molten lead,
By turning its darkened face to its beloved?
But that its glow in the dark night is a lamp to the wanderers,
An inspiration and object of praise to the poets,
A role-model and object of jealousy amongst the stars.'

The Moon Reveals the Sun

Knowledge of the *Moon* reveals the *Sun*
Knowledge of the *parts* reveal the *Source*
The water of the *Sea* does *heal our wounds*
The water of our *tears* does *heal our Souls.*

Absorption in the *Sun* conceals the *Moon*
Absorption in the *Source* conceals the *parts*
Capturing the *Moon* brings Lovers clues
The *Sun's* inner rising *reveals the Hearts*

The Beauty and Majesty of His Love

In seeking His love, if you refuse to face *Its Majesty*, then how can you deserve *Its Beauty*?

Divine Love rips the foundations of the heart and flips the whole downside up, until the darkness surfaces and *the Light prevails*.

Give your form up to the Formless, give your attachment to forms up to the Formless, *till you are informed by the Formless*.

Divine love is not found in pages bound to rot in the earth they came from; but in the depths of the night away from Mankind's eyes; in the chests of Men who have at the drop-of-a-hat *given their every belonging and attribute to their Beloved.* If you cannot do at least that, then give up the garb of the Lovers and speak not another word of it.

Divine Love is not given in exchange for superficial words of sweetness and frivolity. It demands *your head* for ransom; *Its Nectar* won't be tasted until Its Will is rested upon *that head*;

Divine Love is a Secret Gem hidden in the symbol of prostration,
O Allāhu Akbar!

The Friend of Silence

In the presence of a true friend, neither is silence an enemy nor is speech a tyrant.

Silence is not opposed and speech is not forced.

The home of true friendship is built with silence as the grounding *earth* and speech as its supporting *walls* – the *earth* is warm and soft, and the *walls* are built with doors and windows open to the expansive landscapes.

Neither does the air grow stale nor do the eyes grow dull.

Its inhabitants dwell therein *willingly* and are under no compulsion.

Their rent is paid with *love*, and this comes not from their pocket, but from *Divine Grace.*

O Allāh - keep us amongst *Your Sincere Ones,* in this life and the Next.

The Throne of the Heart

Is it any wonder that the bird is capable of *swaying the Souls* with its song whilst these self-proclaimed learned men cannot?

Is it any wonder when the latter is a tongue echoing words on pages while the former is a heart emitting *the music of its Soul*?

The bird does not intend to *change* anyone with its voice. *And yet the hearts are changed.*

It praises its Lord and the space is beautified. It is pleased with Him, and He is pleased with it.

O learned man! Be more like the bird.

Listen to a man only if his words *quake the ground of your core.*

For he, like the bird, has *realised his purpose,* and acts upon it.

For he, like the bird, is *seated on the throne of his heart.*

For he, like the bird, is *the lover of God*; the living, breathing, manifested words of the pages.

And the lovers are the victors.

The Hidden Ones

Wilāya (Sainthood) is not exclusive to fame
There are *Awliyā'* that have come and gone
No one ever knowing their name

Yet all drank from their *Light*
And benefited from their *baraka*
Just as the gardens benefit from the *pouring rain*

It is not by eloquence that these Souls rose
There are *Awliyā'* that have come and gone
With only a handful hearing their voice

Not by their cleverness was it granted
Nor are efforts the source of this gift
No, but it is the *Eternally Merciful's Choice*

The Era of Mercy

How many civilizations have perished through disobedience to Allāh?

How many tyrants have been consumed oppressing the Messengers of Allāh?

How many heedless ones have turned away from the Mercy of Allāh?

And thus deprived their own *Souls* from the Eternal Mercy of Allāh?

Hell means complete veiling from the Mercy of Allāh

In this Era, know that the reason we are *preserved* from being destroyed by the Wrath of Allāh

And that His Mercy so closely envelops even the enemies of Allāh

Is because *Dunya's soil* is being graced by *the Noble Body of Rasūlullāh* ﷺ

The Winged Stranger

If at road's end
Of countless years of toil
You stand in awe
Before your structures raised
Your flourishing pastures sowed
By your tired and blistered hands
Dreamed up by a weary heart
You stand before your lands
A winged strangers appears
Unannounced
Inviting you to his cloud above
Don't harbour regret in your heart
For the hours and effort invested
In a space that meets your feet
Rather
Bestow those archaic structures
To the restless hearted yet to meet
Their winged stranger
For their sincerity still needs proving
Their heart still needs a medium
To color this world with its vision
Sprout those wings

Your birthright
By your new-found soaring Will
Join hands with the new friend
And reach for the sky's palaces
To the abode of higher aspirations

The Two Freedoms

If freedom is: 'Doing whatever *you* like'
Who is '*you*'?
Is it the *you* of *your true Celestial Nature*
That calls you to *the Highest Good*?
Or is it the *you* of lower-worldly nature
That stems from the root of desire?
For in every moment
You answer to either one of the two
Is shamelessness *freedom*?
It is being free from *True Freedom*
That of your *True Nature*
And so it is complete enslavement
To the other *you*
Attached to the worldly lures
What appears outwardly as *freedom*
May actually be a cunning mirage
Cast by enslavement
And what appears outwardly as *enslavement*
May be *a Divine Veil*
Cast upon Its Jewels
Covering Its Secrets in jealousy

O Mindless Critic

O mindless critic -
You approach the open chest
And all you see is the dust settled upon it
Oblivious to the fact
That the worth of the gold and gems
Beneath it is unchanged
By this slight veil
It is your eyes that are filled with dust
O you bereft of discrimination
O mindless critic
You claim to seek wisdom
And yet you approach the men of knowledge
With a vessel full to the brim
With empty analysis and prejudice
And you walk away claiming
They have nothing you don't already know
That is only because
The subtle dimension
In which the meanings they convey travel
Are invisible to eyes engrossed by the tangible
O mindless critic
Drop the books

Be *still*
Be *silent*
In the presence of the Masters

The Heart's Delight

Your physical beauty is drowned out
By your character and actions

To those to whom inner realities
Bring deeper satisfaction

The ones that you'll call to you
Likely those drowned in lower passions

What good will sweetness for the eyes do
When the lower self comes lashing

Your beauty is admirable
But that which *manifests from Light*

As fruits from the inner branches
From the roots of the heart's delight

Your inner purity's a bird
Raising your Soul to untold heights

Your sincerity and humility
Is *a Sun in another's night*

Upon your heart is written
Your honor and dignity is a right

Your righteous intentions keep it living
Your Divine aspiration is a Light

The Oil of Listening

My heart is a broken shard of glass
Reflecting the *Muhammadan Light* ﷺ

This world is bland to the lover's tongue
As the day's a stranger to the night

Don't hold back your light from this moment
In grievance of what you believe you've lost

In full circle *its essence will return*
But this moment won't as it does

Distill the oil of listening
From the blossoming petals of hearing

Helpless in the Beloved's quicksand
Lured in by a fiery yearning

The Rope of Love

The heart is drawn to its roots
Towards the Source of its being

Pulled in by the rope of Love
To that Sea of infinite meanings

The Celestial rains of Mercy
Shower in torrents of healing

This heart we speak of needs not air
Only that Sacred Water for breathing

Every stranger: *kept out of reach*
Of that heart by the sword Love is wielding

Pulled away from trampling hooves
Just as the pure Earth nurtures its seedlings

Everything You Touch

Change is made one heart at a time
Don't undervalue the power in your choice

Everything you touch is transformed
Don't undervalue the power in your voice

The issue is not greed for *Power*
But ignorance of its *Source* and *Reality*

The truth of its *Manifestation*
Its consequences and responsibility

Fire can bake to feed your home
It can also burn it to cinders

Match in hand, do you seek to destroy
Or warm your home through the winter?

Glory in the Wounds

You wind your flame with lovers' words
When will you pen your own story?

When will you crack those wounds open
To find within that same Glory

The poor souls at the Beloved's door
They speak with the same tongue

The air they breathe is Love
They breathe with the same lung

Your Soul is weary of the castles in the sand
It cries for the journey away from the safe shores

It cries for the *Invisible* to lend a hand
Into the unknown oceans to quench its deepest
core

The Light the Night Sows

The Sun keeps shining even with our eyes closed
The Moon keeps waxing even with our blindfolds

Light grows from the very seeds the night sows
A fire that ignites souls, brighter than what minds hold

Time scolds, except those trekking with bright glows
Through the arid, wild deserts of prized souls

Bending with the perpetual plights life might throw
They rise forth in unity that only broken eyes know

The wise grow, always, every breath their life blows
With every bit of awe and innocence a child shows

An intellect that sets apart Gold from rhinestones
Feeding us from their Oceans wherever their rivers might flow

The night sows the Light from which the mind grows
The heart knows, guided by the signs the wise show

Their words are water to the seeds of Light the night holds
The Light the night sows, *journey of the Realised Souls*

Whispers of the Beloved

Whoever caught in the depths of night
The whispers his Beloved made

But he whose neck is outstretched
Merely inches from Its swinging blade?

Sleep starved eyes are quenched
By the sweet waters of Its Fragrance

The slightest mention of Its name
Lights hearts up in Its radiance

How can Its *Name* not saturate
Every fiber of their being

The restless hearted wholly steeped
In remembrance of those *Meanings*?

Where Secrets Are Stored

Give your craft a worldly name
But its reality's much vaster

The essence of action is intention
That inner Light, who is its *Master*?

Let music flow freely
From the Spring of Endless Rivers

Your body is the reed flute
Whose breath makes it so shiver?

The hourglass is emptying
The sands of Destiny, *they pour*

What do you wish to share
Of that heart where secrets are stored?

The Blind Bee

In a flower-filled valley
There was a thirsty bee
In a blind colony
Bees that could not see

Every bee in the colony
Knew not colored vision
But never did it stop them
From collecting their provision

Except the thirsty bee
It could not leap for flight
So its unsighted companions
Would feed it through its plight

One day the elder bees
In their weekly get-together
Had come to the decision
This could not last forever

The verdict was as follows:
The thirsty bee was to be

Left in the valley, lonely
With but the shade of an ancient tree

The bee, perplexed and frantic
Cried through its sleepless nights
It yearned for that sweet nectar
It once thought was its right

The scorching summer heat did not
But aggravate its craving
The buzzing of its fellow bees
Kept its fantasies raving

Collapsed, consumed by its pool of tears
A drop of nectar fell
From a careless bee in the skies above
In the thirsty bee's new well

Overwhelmed by *Ecstasy*
The bee soared to the skies
Singing, '*O with my heart so colored*
What need for these eyes?'

The Winds of Solace

The winds of solace
Bring in their untold melodies

A spirit of renewal
To revive a deep serenity

A placeless voice draws close
And whispers softly '*let it be*'

Like a story told just once
And it was only read to me

The ringing notes of change
I hear what they are telling me

A shelter in the rain
A soft spoken entity

My Home Is Untrodden Path

My home is untrodden path
I search the sand beneath

The gold is always hidden
The sword's silver is sheathed

I am not my Religion
Religion is my Key

Studded with Priceless Gems
Reflecting Eternity

My home is untrodden path
The land, the skies, the seas

My heart is no stranger
To the lonely desert breeze

I don't own my Religion
Religion is a Sea

The forceful die drowning
The patient are set free

اللّٰهُمَّ يا أَكْرَمَ الأَكْرَمِين
إجْعَلْ أَكْرَمَ الصَّلَوَاتِ وَ أَفْضَلَ التَّسْلِيم
عَلَى نَبِيِّنَا الكَرِيمِ طٰهٰ يٰس
صَلَاةً تَكْشِفُ لَنَا بِهَا وَجْهَهُ الكَرِيم
وَ عَلَى آلِهِ وَ أَصْحَابِهِ وَ جَمِيعِ المُرْسَلِين

O ALLĀH - O MOST GENEROUS OF THOSE WHO ARE GENEROUS, BESTOW SWIFTLY THE MOST GENEROUS OF BLESSINGS AND THE MOST GRACIOUS PEACE UPON YOUR GENEROUS PROPHET - ṬĀHĀ, YĀSĪN - A PRAYER THAT UNVEILS TO US HIS GENEROUS COUNTENANCE, AND UPON HIS FAMILY AND COMPANIONS AND THE ENTIRETY OF THE MESSENGERS.

- 'Ṣalāt al-Karam' (The Invocation of Generosity)
by Walid Lounès Bouzerar

﴿سُبْحَانَ رَبِّكَ رَبِّ الْعِزَّةِ عَمَّا يَصِفُونَ ۝
وَسَلَامٌ عَلَى الْمُرْسَلِينَ ۝
وَالْحَمْدُ لِلَّهِ رَبِّ الْعَالَمِينَ ۝﴾

11063219R00042

Printed in Great Britain
by Amazon